THINI
RICH
TO GET
RICH

THINK RICH TO GET RICH

THE FOUR GOLDEN RULES FOR BEING SUCCESSFUL IN BUSINESS

ARCTURUS

Arcturus Publishing Limited
26/27 Bickels Yard
151–153 Bermondsey Street
London SE1 3HA

Published in association with

foulsham

W. Foulsham & Co. Ltd,
The Publishing House, Bennetts Close, Cippenham,
Slough, Berkshire SL1 5AP, England

ISBN-13: 978-0-572-03191-6
ISBN-10: 0-572-03191-2

This edition printed in 2006
Copyright © 2006 Arcturus Publishing Limited

British Library Cataloguing-in-Publication Data: a catalogue record for this
book is available from the British Library

Printed in Egypt

CONTENTS

Foreword

-Why I Write-

When you think about it, 'thinking' is an interesting subject to think about. Thinking is actually something you *can* think about. You can't eat about eating. You can't swim about swimming, but you can think about thinking. I love to think about the way we think, and what we think, and the cause and effect of our thinking. Yet are we so busy we haven't got the time to think? Are we so tired and brain dead that thinking is the last thing we have time to think about? More and more – are we thinking about less and less?

Who Is Thinking For Whom?

Are we allowing others like the media, politicians, religious leaders, parents, teachers, pundits, psychics, celebrities, spin doctors, bosses, friends, even traditions and superstitions, to think for us? Are we being told how we should and must think, and do we accept the thinking of others without thinking for ourselves? A pragmatic thinker is a person who observes himself or herself, other people, and the issues of the world around them, in as practical a way as possible. We strive to think for ourselves, examining the cause and effect of our thinking.

I strive to see things as they really are, not just as I want them to be, or how I have been told they are. I question everything and have a lot of fun doing it. Most people play tennis or racquetball, go boating, go on hikes, or play golf for fun. I think. Life is about the questions, not the answers. The answers always change, but the questions remain the same. Frankly, the more I know, the more I know I don't know. Many times what I thought yesterday, I think is silly today. So I write so I can think more clearly. I want to live life to the fullest with my mind wide open! Thinking is hard: that's probably why most of us enjoy eating so much. If you can't have your 'mind wide open', why not have your mouth that way? I should know!

The Pragmatic Thinker
A few of my commentaries are written tongue in cheek for no other reason than to entertain myself. However, in the main, I am as serious as a heart attack about my

thoughts. I am not looking for followers, fans, or disciples. I'm not that smart or that stupid. I only hope my commentaries make you want to think and help you make thinking a habit. It has been said that we should think 'outside the box'. Most of us don't even think inside the box! Hey, thinking is a good thing! As Albert Einstein said, 'We can't solve problems by using the same kind of thinking we used when we created them.'

So, I try to think. I try to see the world as pragmatically as possible. The Pragmatism Cybrary (cyber library) defines pragmatism as 'a major intellectual movement, which started in America in the late 1800s.' Pragmatists have influenced politics, law, education, religion and every academic discipline. Today, pragmatism is one of the most active fields of American philosophy, and the world's interest in it is still growing. In 1907, William James, a noted pragmatist, described pragmatic thinking, or scientific thinking, by advising us to: 'Grant an idea or belief to be true,' and then question, 'what concrete difference will its being true make in anyone's actual life? How will the truth be realized? What experiences will be different from those which you would obtain if the belief were false? What, in short, is the truth's cash-value in experiential terms?'

As Charles S. Peirce, the founder of pragmatism, put it, 'The pragmatist knows that doubt is an art which has to be acquired with difficulty.' So I doubt everything, especially my own thinking. Truth is always evolving as we evolve. This makes life fun. We are always thinking, whether we want to or not. Think about it . . . pragmatically, of course!

Introduction: Entrepreneurs Wanted!

You are currently reading a book I didn't want to write. Not because I don't enjoy writing – I love to write – but because if you write on the subject of wealth and riches you are sticking your neck out for someone to chop your head off. Rowena Harwood, an old friend's high school English teacher, used to tell her students, 'Your friends are eager to put you down.' This applies even more when you're teaching someone how to get rich and have as much wealth as they want. People are eager to say, 'He's not that rich . . . what does he know about getting rich?' The reason is that you are dealing with a concept that cannot easily be defined. People are quick to say, 'You don't know what rich is,' and maybe I don't. But with that said, I have been forced to come up with a definition that works for me. I consider myself rich when I can do everything in life I want to do, travel and go wherever I want, buy whatever I want, and live wherever I want, in the home I want, driving the car I want, and never, yes never, have to look at my bank balance. That means there would always be plenty of money to cover all the cheques and charges to support my lifestyle. That is my definition of **rich**.

Rich Is A Lifestyle

But **rich** cannot be defined by a figure, only by a lifestyle. If you have to ask if you are rich, you're not. When you are rich, you know it. But by my definition, a person can be rich making $100,000 a year or less, just as they can if they make $100,000,000 a year. The reverse could also be true. A person could be poor making $100,000,000 a year. I can be rich with a lot less than many rich people. I just don't need all the toys they need. After all, the basics of life like food, shelter, and clothing are taken care of on a much lower income: being rich is all about the toys. I can be just as rich and happy living in a $300,000 home with a couple of acres for my horses and riding my Harley Heritage Soft Tail as a friend who drives a $100,000 Mercedes and lives in his million-dollar mansion. That's the great thing about being rich. You are the only one who needs to know. Rich is a lifestyle, attitude and mindset. The other day I was talking to a friend about becoming rich, saying I could be rich making $250,000 a year when he interrupted me and said, 'You've got to be kidding. You can't make $250,000 a year and be rich.' Now this friend has never made more than $20,000 a year, but he was quick to say $250,000 wasn't sufficient to make me rich. I asked him if he had ever made $250,000 a year, and when he replied, 'no,' said, 'When you do, tell me if you feel rich. If you don't, you are right: if you do, I am right! Rich is not a figure, it's a lifestyle.'

Follow The Formula

So as you read this book, try not to confuse a certain income figure with the mindset of being rich. It's **not** the same thing. As a sales, marketing, and advertising consultant and businessman, it has been my pleasure to work with hundreds of self-made, rich business people. Without exception, they **all** followed the same formula for gaining wealth. The Four Pillars of Wealth have been the same for all people who have become rich through running their own business. If you follow the formula of the Four Pillars, you too can become rich. It is not a matter of **if**, it is a matter of **when**! The old wisdom of, 'Go to school, get a job, and get rich,' just isn't true any longer. I would say in most cases it is more likely to be, 'Go to school, get a job, and get poor!' There are few, if any, jobs, that can keep pace with the rising costs of inflation and the increasing numbers of people chasing fewer and fewer opportunities. We live in a technological world whose main objective is to make life easier and faster, while at the same time reducing the need for factories and factory workers. Industrial centres that used to employ more than 20,000 workers may now have fewer than 200, and many factories have closed down completely. More and more people are graduating from college only to become unemployed, or forced to take low-paying, paid-by-the-hour jobs just to pay the rent. Hey, if you don't believe me, just get a degree in philosophy and try to get a job. You can either teach or start mowing lawns, and the funny thing is that mowing lawns can get you rich a lot faster than a career in teaching! That is the reason I am writing this book. I want to help other people become rich, and of course, along the way I will also make more money myself , so I can continue enjoying my own definition of rich, and helping others assure their position of prosperity. Think about it.

The Four Pillars of Wealth

As we get started, let me repeat something I said in the Introduction. 'The Four Pillars of Wealth have been the same for **all** people who have become **rich** through having their own business. If you follow the formula of the Four Pillars, you too can become rich. It is not a matter of **if**, it is a matter of **when**!' If you are an entrepreneur, own your own business, or have the responsibility and accountability to run a business, this book is for you. If you currently work for someone else, and want to make more money without leaving your current employment, starting your own business to earn extra money 'on the side' may be the answer. This book will definitely show you how.

The 'Rich Formula'
One thing I know for sure is that most people want to get rich. Some want power, some want fame, but

almost all of us want money. So I came up with a 'rich formula' that is 100 per cent successful. This formula, when precisely followed, will make you **rich**. Most of us have been told, 'If you work hard, you will make money.' That is true, but the question is, how much money? I have seen people who work hard at McDonalds, Wal-Mart, Taco Bell, Ace Hardware, or in real estate, insurance, advertising, training horses, cooking, and building homes. They work between 10 and 12 hours a day, six or seven days a week, and never have two nickels to rub together at the end of the month. So, looking at this in a pragmatic way, just working hard and long certainly doesn't ensure you will get rich. Some say that the key to getting rich is to 'work smart', not 'hard.' I think I know what they mean when they say that. This 'work smart' concept has been explained to me as doing the things that are **important**, not just the things that are **urgent**. I will admit that this is definitely a step in the right direction, but one step is not enough to get rich. To come up with a real formula to make money and keep money, I have been looking at and evaluating all the rich people I know. Back in science class, we all learned that the formula for water is H_2O, or two hydrogen atoms and one oxygen atom. HO_2 is quite different. The formula for water is what it is and you can't change it. So what is the pragmatic formula for getting rich?

The State of Being Rich

Now, when I say 'get rich' I am not talking about 'doing well', 'getting by', 'doing OK', or 'doing fine'. I am talking about being *rich* – that point where money doesn't rule your life, but you rule money. That point in life when you do the things you want to do, when you want to do them, without worrying about how you will afford to do them. I don't need to tell you when you are rich; you will know when you are rich. It is like someone asking you, 'How will I know when I have arrived?' If you have to ask, you haven't. If you have to ask if you are rich, you're not. Being rich is not a number; it is a state of mind and a lifestyle. But believe me, when you are . . . you know it.

So here is the pragmatic formula that will make you rich. The system is based on four giant Pillars of Wealth. Using one or two of the pillars will help you make more money, but if you use all four, you will get rich. So don't say you don't need one of them. You need all four pillars to be rich. Each of the pillars has a rule associated with it. Follow the rule . . . get rich. It is that simple.

First Rule: Twice As Good At Half The Price
The rule of the first pillar is, 'Whatever you decide to do . . . **Be twice as good at half the price!**' Now that was easy, wasn't it? You could have come up with that simple rule. What I mean here is that regardless of the business or service you offer, don't offer it for just half the price but not quite as good: No! It must be twice as good as the competition . . . but at **half the price**. You figure out how to do that. Wal-Mart and Target sell the same merchandise you can buy at other stores, but it costs a whole lot less. They figured out how to do that and even though some people hate to shop there, they still do. Sure, Wal-Mart puts the 'little guy' out of business, but that is what capitalism is all about. Capitalism is just another name for the War of Businesses. But I digress. It used to be said that if you wanted to make a million dollars, you should build a better mousetrap. That may be true if the better mousetrap cost less than the old standard mousetrap. But, if the new and better mousetrap costs twice as

much, then you have a whole lot of selling to do to convince people that your mousetrap is indeed better and worth the extra money. I will write more about this concept of twice as good at half the price later in this book. I will show you how to be twice as good, and how important your price point is. You may not be able to be half the price, but perception is reality, so keep reading. As for now, remember, less is always best when it comes to the mind of man. We are greedy souls. Sure, quality sells, but sell twice the quality at half the price and you will sell much more, and you will sell it easier and faster. You are on your way to getting rich. But it doesn't stop there.

Second Rule: Share Your Knowledge
The second pillar's rule is: **'Share your knowledge.'** What this means is to teach others how to do what you do. In other words, if you are a great landscaper, teach others to do what you do until they are as good as you are, or better. If you are a great builder of children's play houses, teach others to build children's play houses as well as, or better than, you build them. Here's another way of looking at this: as soon as you are the best basketball player on the court, teach

someone to be as good as or better than you and start coaching. You can never get rich if all your personal time, energy and resources are tied up in 'doing the do.' You can't get rich if you are so busy doing landscaping that you don't have time to get more business. As soon as you can see that you are 70 to 80 per cent busy, start sharing your knowledge. Don't wait until you are so busy that you don't have time to share your knowledge. This is important.

Third Rule: Share The Wealth

The third pillar's rule is: **'Share the wealth.'** What this means is that you have to be willing to let go of the lion's share of the money so you can make more money. Make others rich so you can become rich. It is better to get 25 to 50 per cent of a large sum of money, than to have 100 per cent of a small sum of money. Share your knowledge (Pillar Two) and share your wealth (Pillar Three) and start making your money on the quantity and the quality of your work. However, you are not going to be doing this quality work. You have taught as many people as are necessary to get the work done, and for their work you are willing to share the wealth.

Fourth Rule: Stop Doing The Do

The fourth pillar's rule is: **'You have to be willing to stop doing the do, and only work at getting more do to do.'** In other words, you have to be willing to stop doing landscaping, or whatever your business is, and spend most of your time getting more jobs for your people to do. This means you have to be willing to sell your services and stop doing them. This is the easiest thing to teach and the hardest rule to follow. You need to be the president of 'hungry artists.' However, you don't want to be a hungry artist yourself. If you loved to paint, and even if you made money selling your paintings, you can't paint any longer. You can teach people to paint, and pay them to paint, but you can't paint yourself. Instead, you spend your time selling the paintings produced by the hungry artists. You have to be willing to stop doing your business, and instead concentrate on getting more business. And it doesn't stop there. Soon you will hire others and share your knowledge again, and show them how to get more business, like you have been doing, and then they will get more and more business so your people can make more and more money, because you shared with them the knowledge of how to do this. Now you are king in the counting house, counting all your money, and how did you get there?

1 – You were twice as good at half the price.
2 – You shared your knowledge and taught people to do what you do so they could make money too.
3 – You shared the wealth, keeping only 25 to 50 per cent of the profits and paying your people the rest.
4 – You stopped doing your business and started getting more business.

At some point you won't even sell any more, others will do this for you, allowing them to make a rewarding living while you live in rich land. Being rich may not make you any happier, but it will allow you to stop worrying about money and may enrich your life through guiding others so they can make money, too. One thing's for sure, if you have never been rich, don't try to tell me that money doesn't matter. For example, it may not matter to you right now whether you can go to Hawaii and bask in the sun on the white sands at the Grand Waialea Resort. However, once you have been there, it will matter, and you will want to share it with your family and friends. Those who have 'been there and done that' will know what I mean. Those who haven't may say they don't care, but they should care. And so it is with being rich. When you are rich, you want others to be rich, too. It's that good. Remember, being rich is not a number – it's a state of mind and a lifestyle. Only you will know when you have arrived at that rich state of mind. Think about it.

2

Pillar One:

Twice as Good at Half the Price

Being twice as good at half the price is one of those concepts that is easy to say but really hard for most people to do. This is because people can claim that their business or service is twice as good, but can they prove it? People can say it's half the price, but can they prove that? Talking the talk is a lot easier than walking the walk. So let's take some time to make sure that we understand the reasons for the first pillar.

The Importance Of Clients

It is on this pillar that the building of your personal wealth rests. There are two main reasons why your business must be twice as good at half the price. First, sales are much easier to make. Second, clients stay with you longer. When people want you more than you want them, because you are twice as good at half the price, *selling* becomes a simple matter of *explaining* your business. You don't have to be the world's greatest sales person. You don't have to know the attention, interest, conviction, desire and closing steps. You don't have to know a trial close from a buying signal. All you have to do is tell potential customers what your product or service does, and why it is twice as good at half the price, and customers and clients will be begging you instead of you begging them. If there is a need for your service or product, and if people are willing to pay for it, then selling it will be much, much easier and clients will stay with you longer when you are **twice as good at half the price**.

Keeping Your Clients
You see, once a sale is made, especially in a service business, you have to make sure that your clients don't leave you. Selling to a client is a lot easier than keeping a client. Clients are fickle. They'll just wake up one morning and for no good reason, they'll decide that they want to leave you to try someone else. However, let's say that you are in the landscaping business and you mow lawns for residential customers. One day your crew doesn't do everything exactly perfect for one of your clients. Let's say they didn't trim one of the bushes exactly right, so your client

comes home from work after a stressful day and gets out of the car and spots the not-so-perfect bush. She wants to fire you right then and there. She goes right to the phone and starts calling other landscaping services only to find that they don't provide all the services your company does and that the other companies are twice as expensive. All of a sudden she cools down and says, 'It was just a bad day. They always do a great job. They will do better next time,' and you still have a client. So, that is the strategy behind **twice as good at half the price**. You see, if you are as good at the same price, your clients have a choice. If they don't use you, they can choose from a list of other companies who provide the same type of service or product. They don't have to stay with you. But when your clients ask themselves, 'If not you, then who?'- and there's no answer, no other 'who' – then the probability of your clients leaving you is slight. Greed is such a wonderful motivator for clients to stay with you. Everyone wants a product or service that is better than the competition and costs less than the competition. Again, selling to clients and keeping clients is one of the keys of getting rich and staying rich.

The Easy Life

I was talking to a friend of mine about what she wanted out of life. Of course, like most, she wanted peace of mind and to be rich. I asked her what she meant by peace of mind and she said to stop worrying so much about money. I said that kind of peace of mind is easy, it is the other kinds of peace of mind that are hard to come by. Anyway, she said that if she could make $250,000 a year, she would consider herself rich. So I asked her what she was going to do to make $250,000 a year, and she said, 'I don't want to do anything. I just want to win the lottery or have my husband make that much. I want to cook for my friends, and have enough money to do what I want to do when I want to do it, whether that is travelling or staying at home, and just live life free from the worry of not having enough money.' Well, count me in too.

Get Rich Quick?

I would like to discuss the issue of wanting to get rich quickly and the effect of that kind of thinking. It seems kind of silly that most of the people I talk to want to win the lottery and live out the rest of their lives doing nothing. But it is impossible to do nothing. Even sitting contemplating your navel is doing something. So, even if we win the lottery we have to do something. That is why, if you possibly can, you should start your business doing something you really enjoy. This just makes life more fun. When you have a passion for the something you are doing to make money, it makes the whole experience of working more like playing. It would be hard for me to have a landscaping business even if I could make a million dollars a year doing it. I have no passion for mowing lawns and trimming bushes. Landscaping is work to me. But, on the other hand, having a business in sales, advertising and marketing is a real passion in my life. My point is that you need to start a business doing something you really enjoy and something you really have a passion for. It also really helps if you are good at what you do. I could never make a living doing oil paintings . . . unless stick figures come back into style!

What To Do To Get Rich?

Most of us won't win the lottery, so we had better think of what we will *do* to get rich. Just wanting to be rich doesn't work or we would all be rich. I have never met a person who wanted to be poor. I have never met a person who wanted to worry about money. Don't be silly! We all want to be rich. So, what are *you* going to do to become rich? What is it that you can do twice as well and at half the price?

Picking A Business

It helps to pick a business that people want, and that they will be willing to pay money for you to do the service, or to buy the product you sell. No matter how wonderful you think a business is, if people don't want your services, you don't have a business. Try to have a business that has as big a universe of prospective customers as you can. You might be really talented at snail watching, but I don't know a lot of people that would pay you to do that for them. The best way to choose your business is to pick something that has a great deal of competition, which means there is a great demand for the service, and then study the leader in the industry. Know the Big Number One better than you know your children. Know what they charge, what services they offer, who their suppliers are, what their best accounts are, what makes people motivated to go to them, how many people they have working for them, and so on. The point is that if you don't *know* the competition, you can't *beat* the competition. After all, business is war. Most of us don't kill each other any more to take away each other's land, homes or possessions, we just beat them in business. If you don't know the competition and how they think, what they do, and how you can do it better than they can do it, you cannot form a strategy to beat them at their own game.

Same Service . . . Twice As Good . . . Half The Price
Once you know the answers to these questions, it is simple. All you have to do is offer the same services as Big Number One and do them **twice as well at half the price**. You have the advantage. Big Number One won't even notice that you are taking business from them. They will be too big to notice. You are David and they are Goliath. They will think it is silly that you are even trying. But you can be silly all the way to the bank. When your business is truly twice as good at half the price, clients will come to you. You just have to let them know that your business exists and clients and customers will beat a path to your door. We will talk more about this issue of marketing and sales later. But for now, you must know that you are in sales. You will

never stop selling your services until you complete Pillar Four.

Concentrating On Quality

For now, concentrate on the business you have, or are creating, and on how you can truly be twice **as good at half the price**. If you can't charge half the price, come as close to that figure as you can, but there is never any excuse for not being twice as good. Quality service alone can make you twice as good. When you are really twice as good at half the price and are getting more and more business every day, you are ready to 'share the knowledge.' Think about it.

3

Pillar Two:
Share the Knowledge

Once you have a business that you know has plenty of demand and you are doing the do of the business, making money, refining your services, beating the competition, and 60 to 70 per cent of your time is taken up in servicing the customers and clients you currently have, you are ready for Pillar Two. This is where you share your knowledge of your business and teach someone else to be as good as you are.

Or do you? No! You must teach them to be *better* than you are at your own business. The reason you start this process when 70 to 80 per cent of your time is taken up in servicing your current client base is because if you don't start now, you'll miss the window of opportunity. You will soon be 100 per cent busy just taking care of business, and you will have no time to sell your services. Remember you can't get out of sales, or you are done for. You will hit a plateau and be unable to progress to the next stage of the business.

You are the key to the next step. The business needs you and you need time.

Don't Be Irreplaceable

Now, I am not going to say you won't be making money . . . you will. But you won't be able to grow your business because you will not have time to grow it. You have now created a business that is twice as good at half the price and you have more business than you know what to do with, and at this point you will think no one can replace you. Only you can do what you do. If you stop servicing your clients and customers, they will leave you.

At this point you will want to hire someone to sell your services so you will have time to service your clients, and the reason is because you are so darned important to your customers. Stop this stupid thinking. The reason your customers come to you is because you are twice as good at half the price. You are a nice person, but your customers would leave you and go to another company if the other company were twice as good at half your price. Remember, you can never be 'as good' at the 'same price' or your clients will leave you. You are the key to new sales, new customers, and new business. No one, at least right now, can sell your business as well as you can. No one! I know that most of you will fight me on this. You think that you are such a great 'mower of lawns' that no one would ever be able to mow lawns as well as you, but believe me, if you are willing to **share the knowledge** you will find someone who will be better than you. Sad but true; you are replaceable. You are going to work yourself out of a job and teach someone else to be better than you.

Don't Do: Teach!

The best way to do this is to think of yourself as a mentor. You are going to advise someone to be better than you are at doing your business. This means that you are going to have to be a good teacher. This will take some patience for a lot of us. Just the fact that we are entrepreneurial people means we could be described as loners, and we like things done our way. It is here that I don't want you to confuse a system with a method. If you do, you will micro-manage your understudy to death. The reason I use the word 'understudy' is because the person you are advising is an understudy to you in just the same way as the people who understudy leading actors on the stage.

An understudy knows all the lines, all the songs, all the staging, all the costume changes, all the cues, and all the scenes. But no two actors perform the same part in exactly the same way. The lines may be the same, but the delivery is unique and distinct to each individual actor. That is what I mean when I talk about 'systems' and 'methods'. A system is a way the company must be run. A method is how each person decides to do it, or work within the systems that you have set up. Teach the systems, policies, rules, and so on, and let your understudy decide how to best get the job done. Remember, just like the stage actor, the lines are the same, but the actor interprets the lines and delivers them in a way that is uniquely theirs. You want to concentrate on systems and expectations, but let your understudy decide how to make the systems work while achieving your desired results or expectations. You don't care *how* the results are achieved as much as you care that the results *are* achieved.

Learn Smart
Systems are the safeguards you have set up in your business that ensure the job is done right and that you

will make money. You came up with these systems while you were creating the business. You came up with the best systems through a lot of trial and error. You know your systems work because you are doing them and because you have 'already made all the mistakes'. Sure, there will be more mistakes, but you know enough of the things not to do that you can now make money not making those mistakes again.

It is rather like when you learned as a child not to touch the hot stove. You could believe your mother when she said, 'Don't touch the hot stove or you will get burned', or you could just touch the hot stove and get burned. The result would be the same in the end: you wouldn't touch the hot stove again. However, one way is learning the hard way, the other way is learning the smart way.

If your understudy is smart, she or he will learn from your mistakes and not touch the hot stove. Thus mistakes and errors are our friends as long as we learn from them. The more mistakes you make, and consequently refrain from making again, the more successful you will be at your business. Not trying will ensure that you don't succeed. Just think of it as a game that you must win at all costs.

Teach Smart

So, now that you have learned from a lot of hard work, mistakes and successes . . . **share the knowledge**. Wouldn't it be terrible if all scientists had to begin anew with only the knowledge of Aristotle, who is called the first scientist? Thank goodness in the world of science there is a lot of shared knowledge. Sharing the knowledge allows your understudy to start years ahead of where you started. Part of getting rich and staying rich is to share the knowledge so that others can become better than you by having the advantage of learning from your mistakes. Become the world's greatest teacher. Don't stay the world's greatest landscaper. It is time for you to move on, and just like Aristotle, share the knowledge. Even though the process is painful, the results are so profitable that it's worth it.

Teaching requires you to examine every system you currently carry out. Put them in writing when at all possible, and expect your understudy to learn so much that there comes a day when they will teach you . . . that is, if you wanted to learn more about doing your business. But you won't want to learn more about mowing a lawn or writing advertising copy or selling a home; you have been there, and done that. You are in the business of selling your products and services and teaching, and when the student becomes more knowledgeable than the teacher . . . get ready to get rich!

'Jump In The Water'

The best way to teach is the old, 'Throw them in the pool and wait for them to scream for help!' I don't mean that you don't give them any information, of course you will. You wouldn't want a doctor just out of college to give you open-heart surgery. You don't want a pilot just out of flying school to jump into a 747 and fly you to Japan. That's why doctors out of college work for years before they step into an operating theatre as consultant surgeons. That's why trainee pilots just sit in the cockpit for a while observing. You want to teach your understudy by giving them the opportunity to watch you and listen to you. Then they 'jump in the water' while you watch, and yell for help if they get into trouble. You want your understudy to do the do while you are right there, close at hand to save them should they fail. But you don't want to stay there as master and saviour for very long. You have to give your understudy the opportunity to fail. We learn much more by failing than by having someone telling us each small step we must take along the way.

Take A Back Seat

So, advise by having them shadow you for a while as you do the do. Then have them do the work while you watch and help when needed. Then comes the hardest part . . . don't show up for work. This will kill you. But in order to really help the understudy learn the most; you must walk away and see what happens. Let them fail. Let them succeed. But let them do the do without you. 'When the student is ready, the teacher will appear.' As long as the understudy thinks they know, they will have no questions for you. It is not until you let your understudy go out on stage without you that they will have questions. We can only learn if we want to know. Failure brings out the questions in all of us. So answer the questions and encourage your understudy to keep asking them. Make your understudy see that you love it when they ask questions. Don't make them feel stupid for asking or they will not ask. Make them feel smart for asking questions and your understudy will become the star and you can sit back and collect your riches. If you always have to be the star you can never be rich. Stars make good money, but it is the producers, studios and distributors who get rich. You don't have to be the best landscaper, let your understudy be that, but you should want to be the richest person who owns a landscaping business.

You can't become rich by doing the do. Share the knowledge and then you are ready to share the wealth. Think about it.

4

Pillar Three:
Share the Wealth

This is when your business really begins to get fun. However, in order for you to get rich you are going to have to suppress your natural desire to be greedy. You are going to have to make a commitment to someone else to help them become wealthy. You are going to have to **share the wealth**, and that won't be easy. You see, most employers try to pay their people as little as possible so the employer can make as much as possible. In fact, just the opposite is true. You need to pay your people as much as possible if you want to get rich. People are your most valuable resource. The people who work with and for you have more to do with you getting rich than you do. You need to try to give them as much as you possibly can in salary, bonuses, benefits and freedom, and just when you think that you have given them enough, give them more! I want you to pay them twice as much as they could earn doing the same job for someone else. Right, that's what I said: 'Pay them **twice as much!**'

Why Pay Twice As Much?

There are two reasons for this. First, if you pay them twice as much as they could earn anywhere else, then even on their very worst day when they want to tell you where to shove their job, they will think twice before doing so. Where are they going to go? If they leave you and look for work with one of your competitors, they will have to cut their pay in half, not to mention losing all the benefits. You want them to thank their lucky stars each day that you are as crazy as you are for paying them so much.

Secondly, you want to pay your people twice as much as they could get anywhere else doing the same thing so you don't have to go back to Pillar Two and 'share the knowledge' again. Training and teaching take time. The last thing you want to do is step down and look for another person to whom you have to teach the business. Time is money, and if you are going to be rich you need your people to stay with you forever. If you teach your people well, give them the freedom they need to incorporate their own methods to achieve your desired results, and pay them twice as much as the competition, they will be with you forever. They will even think twice about going out on their own and starting their own business. Why should they? They can have all the advantages of making lots of money and none of the risks that come with running their own business. They are happy to go home at night and forget about you and your business. You, on the other hand, never stop thinking about your business. Your business is your baby and it needs tender loving care 24/7. Being an entrepreneur is interesting. You would think that everyone would want to be an entrepreneur, but no. Very few of us want the responsibility, the headaches, the hassle and the risk that we entrepreneurs love! It gives us a reason to get up in the morning. It's all about the game! We love the game of getting rich and even the bad days are the best days compared with having to work for someone else. Not all employers are as wonderful as you are.

Sharing The Wealth
Now let's talk a little about how to share the wealth. The best way is to pay your people a guaranteed salary that is twice as good as anywhere else and then give

them a 'piece of the pie.' I don't care if you give someone ten times the average salary for their job, it is never enough. Everyone wants a piece of the action. These bonuses and incentives should be given in two ways.

Pay A Percentage

First you should share the wealth by giving your key people a percentage of the gross net monthly profits. Immediate gratification is important when training animals and there is nothing more animal than a human. We want our rewards now. Secondly, you should pay them for the business they bring in. This gives them an incentive to sell, and you want that. You want your people always to be thinking how they can increase the bottom-line profits. Having them 'feel' a part of the profits helps you in two ways. They will always be thinking about keeping the costs down and the profits high. When you only pay on the gross billings and not the gross net profit, there is no incentive for them to save you money.

You are actually encouraging your people to spend money to make money. You don't want a high grossing company with a small profit margin. You want a high gross net profit company. You are in the business to make money, not spend money. Be careful you don't confuse gross profit or billings with gross net profit. You can spend gross net profit, you can't spend gross profit. Pay two types of bonuses; one on the gross net profit of the entire company and one on their personal profit contribution to the company. You decide how much you can give, but when in doubt, give them more!

Spend Money To Make Money

Now let's go back to you . . . the greedy one. I told you this pillar would not be easy. You will say things to yourself like, 'Hey, why am I paying them so much? After all, I was the one who started this company. I was the one who suffered to pay the bills to get this business going. I was the one who laid awake at night worrying about how I was going to make ends meet. I was the one who worked 18-hour days for three years. They didn't worry about their pay. They didn't have to come to work at 6:00 am and get home at midnight. They didn't miss all of their kid's football games. They just came to work, did their job, got their big fat pay cheque, and went home to drink beer and fall asleep in front of the TV.' Yep, that's what you will think, but don't get caught in the trap. Sure you worked hard. Sure you had many sleepless nights. Sure you pay your people a big fat pay cheque, but they are now making you rich, so you don't have to worry about money and you can drive your fancy cars, and live in your big houses, and travel the world, and work when you want and where you want or not at all. Your people are the reason you have the wonderful rich life you have and all they want for giving you all the wonderful rich things of life is a big fat pay cheque. Give them theirs and you can have yours! You must give in order to get. You must lose in order to find. You must pay a lot in order to make a lot. This is an indisputable law of the universe. Don't ask me how or why this law works . . . it just does. I don't know how and why electricity works, but I sure know how to use it. The more you give the more you get . . . so **share the wealth**. Give till it hurts. It's such a great, rich pain. Think about it.

5

Pillar Four:
Stop Doing the Do

At this point, you know where we're going next. You have created a business that is twice as good at half the price. You have taught a person, or people, to do your job . . . and better. You are willing and able to share the wealth and you understand the reason for each of the four pillars. Now it is time for you to follow the instruction of the hardest of the four pillars. Here is where most people fall off the boat. The reason this is so hard is fear. You have the ever-present fear that your business will really fall apart if you don't do the do. More than that, you really enjoy doing the do. You love the power and the adoration you get from being the boss and running your company. You adore the perks, the clients, the title, having a place to go to in the morning called the office. But now it is time to let go of all that and stop doing the do, and that is hard.

What's In A Name?

You would think that telling you to stop working would be a great comfort. After all, most people look forward to the time when they don't have to work. Most people look forward to this thing we call retirement only to find out that retirement kills more people than it helps, and statistics show that a good percentage of men die just a couple of years after they retire. Perhaps they're just old and worn out, but I think that a great deal of living has to do with having a reason for being. When you give up your business, you quickly discover that you have given up your reason for being. We have worked so long to give our lives value because of *what* we do, rather than *who* we are, that our jobs and our businesses become who we are. As silly as that may seem, it is true for most men and women that what they do becomes who they are. If you ask someone to tell you about themselves, they will usually start with what they do for a living or what they used to do. 'I am an advertising executive.' 'I am a cowboy.' 'I am a retired businessman.' 'I am a wife and mother.' 'I am a salesman.' 'I am a stockbroker.' The list goes on and on. We give our lives value by what we do. So when I ask you to stop doing the do and give up your titles like

C.E.O., president, king and benevolent dictator, and just be Bill, Nancy, Larry or Tom . . . this is like giving up your entire world of worth. You are a nothing. . . and nothing is good. But 'nothing' is not easy. You can only truly get rich when you stop doing the do and **let the do happen.**

Letting Others 'Do The Do'

Most people make this transition from 'someone' to 'no one' by continuing to sell the do, and that's all right. You can sell your services and products until you die if you want to, but remember that at some point you should have people working for you that only sell so you don't have to. Yes, I am saying that the day must come when the only thing you do is go into the counting house and count all your money. But remember, you don't take any of the glory or adoration for owning a very profitable company or companies. You are just you and all the glory goes to your people. Let others be the C.E.O., president and even chairman of the board. You just own the company and count your money. You have to move out of the office and work from home. If you are there, your people look to you to be responsible. If you aren't there, your people have to become responsible and accountable. This is the only way to be truly free and rich. If you have hired, advised, trained, educated, consulted and nurtured your key people, they will do the do better than you. So why do they need you? They don't! They need you to keep out of the way and let them make you money. You have taught them how to do this. But, there again, it won't be easy because most entrepreneurs love to micromanage. They love to have their hands on everything. I don't care if it is buying towels and toilet paper, they want to do it. Entrepreneurs love to be in control and love to be loved. So when I say that this final pillar is the hardest for an entrepreneur to do, I mean it. Being nothing and doing nothing is hard work. I have a sign on my desk that says, 'I want my companies and the people who work for my companies to get as much done today as can possibly be done *without me doing anything*! It is the only way my companies and my people can grow.'

Show Me The Money!
Yes, there is another way we entrepreneurs can deal with the 'nothing' issue. We normally set up new businesses and start the four pillars process all over

again, but the second time is so much easier. We know all the mistakes not to make. We know the type of people to hire and teach. We know and understand the importance of the four pillars . . . and we love the game of making money. We are addicted to the game of making money! But instead of standing in the spotlight we stay in the shadows, and allow others to bask in the glory and enjoy the applause and recognition. Our only mantra is 'show me the money.' Think about it.

6

The Many Faces of Sales

Sales are the life-blood of your company and yet, in most companies, they are given little attention. It gets back to the choice of doing that which is most important or that which is most urgent. We tend to do the most urgent things, and those that are most important are left until we have time to attend to them. Often that time never comes. We are always so busy resolving crises that doing the most important thing, selling, gets shoved aside until everything else is done. But everything else is never done!

Make Those Calls!
So, the first thing you must do is **make sales urgent**. The way you do this is to set an appointment to do sales. The best time is at 10:00 am. You have had a couple of hours to get your day going, yet you still have the energy to make your calls. Your prospects are the same. They need a couple of hours to sort things

out so they have time to talk to you. So set a permanent appointment with yourself and never cancel it. You will be keeping this appointment for many years. If it is at 10:00 am each day from Monday to Friday, you will be on the phone calling, and you will continue until you have made 20 calls. That's all, just 20 calls. You won't talk to 20 people; you will just make 20 calls. You will probably only talk to two people, but you will still make 20 calls.

I call this the 'tick mark' method of selling. You know, four straight vertical lines and another horizontal line through them equalling five. You will make four of these five-stroke tick marks a day, totalling 20 tick marks, or 20 calls. If you do this every Monday to Friday of your life you will have more business than you will know what to do with, and you will have to keep hiring people to help you do the do. Remember, eventually this is all you will do . . . and then ultimately you will even hire a person to do this. This method has never failed. Just do it.

Speak To The Decision-Maker
When calling a businessman, the first person you will reach is normally a person you don't want to talk to –

a receptionist or secretary whose job is to act as watch-dog for their boss and keep unwanted calls away from them. That's why you may only talk to two people out of 20. These people are good at their jobs. They consider you as the enemy. Bosses hate sales calls and you are a sales call. So it is the secretary's job to say, 'Send us any information you may have, and we will get back to you.' That is just what you don't want to do. Sending information is the long, long road to success. It is called running up and down the field and never putting any scores on the scoreboard. It makes you feel you are doing something worthwhile, but it doesn't get the job done. You have got to talk to the decision-makers and only the decision-makers and then **give** before you **take**. So when you do talk to the decision-maker, you ask them if it would be all right for you to send them something. (Yes, you can send something as long as you've spoken to them first.) That's all. Just ask their permission to send them something. We operate on the principle of the first time they talk to you they hate you, the second time they talk to you they tolerate you, and the third time they talk to you they start to like you. So, that being the case, the first time you talk to them, give them something and make it easier for them to say yes than no. Then just say you will ring in a few days and ask what they thought about the materials you sent. You then call back in two or three days and just ask them if they got the information. Don't ask them what they thought about it, or if they want to talk to you about anything else. Just ask them if they got the information. If they didn't get the information, they will tell you, and you can send it out again. If they did get the information they will also tell you. Don't ask them if they have read it, just say, 'I just wanted to make sure you got it. I will call you back in a couple of days when you have had time to look it over . . . How would Wednesday be for you?' At this point they will say one of three things: either that that will be fine, or that another day would be better, or that they will call you back. Whatever they say . . . just reply, 'That will be great!' This is not a time to say, 'No, I will call you!' even though you know they are unlikely to call you back. Just say, 'Great!' and wait a couple of days before calling them back. Always keep the ball in your court, or you may be waiting a long time for it to come back to you.

Meet The Client

So now you have talked to your prospective client twice: once to ask permission to send them some materials about your product or service, and once to see if they received the information. Remember, if they received the information and have seen or read it, they will tell you. So if they want to talk on the second call . . . go for it. However, if they don't want to talk on the second call . . . don't worry about it. You still have a couple of calls and visits up your sleeve. So a couple of days after the second call, you ring them back and this time you say, 'Hey, have you had a chance to read the materials I sent you?' At this point they will say yes or no. If they say yes, you say, 'So what did you think?' and they will tell you, and then just talk, answer questions, and so on. But you don't want to **sell** over the phone. It is not a good sale in most cases. What you want is to **meet** your prospect face-to-face. So regardless of whether the client has read your materials, you reply in the same way. You say, 'No problem, but . . . I would like to meet you and I was wondering if I might come over on Wednesday at 10 am?' The client at this point will start to wriggle a little, but remember you have spoken to them a couple of times before and sent them materials and they are starting to feel a little obliged to you, so 50 per cent of the time they will say yes. It is at these face-to-face appointments that the sale is made. When you meet your prospect what will you talk about? Will it be the weather, sports, politics or religion? No! You will talk about **your business**. Just talk. Don't sell. Just talk! Tell the prospect why you are twice as good at half the price. And if you are twice as good at half the price, believe me, you will sell to at least 50 per cent of the people you meet face-to-face. If you can supply what your prospects need, and they are used to paying twice as much for it, you don't have to sell. Just talk to them and tell them your story and you will make the sale. Your prospects will be asking *you* for the contract.

Now, this is where we remind you of numbers again. Of the 20 calls you make every day, only two people will talk to you. Of the two people who talk to you, only one will become a prospect. Out of five prospects, only one will be a good prospect. Out of two good prospects, only one will become a client or customer. It's all numbers. Now if you are a super salesperson your numbers may be better, but even if you are the worst salesperson in the world, the numbers will not let you down. You will make sales if you just do the numbers! Just 20 calls a day will give you all the sales you want. The rest of the numbers take care of themselves.

The How and the Why

So now that you know the **how** and the **why** and the **importance** of sales, in the next chapter I will present to you a system used by everyone, not just entrepreneurs. I want you to learn how things are really created, especially successful businesses. This principle or system is very seldom talked about, but everyone uses it whether they do so consciously or not. Knowing how to use it will greatly increase the speed at which riches come to you. Think about it.

7

Create and Wait

Anyone who knows me knows that I hate any kind of hocus-pocus. I love to observe life through a practical, pragmatic and scientific way of thinking. I don't understand the pervasive thinking behind such things as miracles. To me, a miracle is something that happens about 50 per cent of the time. Those ain't great odds. I resist begging and pleading with God for a miracle to happen. To say there is a lot I don't understand about how things work in this world would be an understatement. There are certainly thousands of laws that are alive and well in the universe that I have yet to discover. Some of us find these laws just by living, some discover the laws through religion, some through thinking and observing, and some learn these laws of universal order through scientific experimentation. Pragmatically and scientifically thinking, we are looking to call a law a law when it is 100 per cent predictable. It's not good enough for me if a law only works 50 per cent of the time. If H_2O was only water 50 per cent of the time that's not good enough to call it a truth or a predictable law that I can count on when I'm thirsty.

Create And Wait

So, that said, here I go writing about a kind of hocus-pocus that, for me, has an outcome that is 100 per cent predictable. For me, this principle works, and I have never known it to fail. Yet when you first hear of this universal law you will think that I have lost my mind. The fact is I have found my mind! I call the law **create and wait**. It's a little like Napoleon Hill's statement, 'Whatever the mind can conceive and can believe, it can achieve.' Now, I know that what I am about to tell you will sound too simple. I know that this will sound too easy. I know that this will sound too much like hocus-pocus for most people, but it isn't! Its 100 per cent predictability makes it a basic and fundamental law of life. If you want something . . . anything . . . all you have to do is create and wait and be willing to act when the window of opportunity opens. As sure as night follows day, the window of opportunity will open. But you have to be ready to jump in as soon as it opens, because the window will slam shut quickly and if it does, it will be nearly impossible to get it to open again.

The basic principle is just this: things must be created spiritually or mentally before they can be manifested physically. The mind has to create the object of our desire before that object will physically manifest itself. But that said, creation is not wishing for something to happen, or hoping for something to happen, or even wanting something to happen. Creation is hard work. You have to train your mind to create and hold on tightly to the thought of your creation while all the time knowing that your creation will be made manifest physically while you do nothing. Again, all you have to do is **create and wait** for your window of opportunity to open. I am not sure how this principle works, or why it always works, but it does. One thing is for sure, the mind never sleeps. You may go to sleep, but your mind keeps on working. Let me give you an example of one of the first times I knew I was using this law of create and wait.

Creation Begins In The Head

I had used the principle all my life, as most people do,

but I was unaware of it. About 15 years ago I bought a new house for my family. It was one of only a couple of homes built in the community at the time. This new home was on an acre of horse property. There was no landscaping, just earth and weeds everywhere. Almost every day I would go outside at the back of my home and just stand there and look at the land for an hour or so. After seeing me do this for several days, my wife asked what I was doing, and I told her, 'I am creating my fences.' She said, 'You mean you are planning where to put your fences?' and I replied, 'It is more like I am creating my fences. I am standing here seeing the fences for my horses, the arena, the gates, the shaded areas; seeing our kids riding and laughing, seeing the horses drinking from the troughs, and creating the hitching posts, the cement washing areas, the hay barn, and the tack house. I can actually see the fences. To me all these things are as real as real.'

The Window Of Opportunity

Now, to a normal person this creating would seem really stupid. But to me, spending time creating by actively thinking about my creation, planting it firmly in my mind, was (and now is) as normal as normal can be. The funny thing about creation is that the more you create, the easier it is to have your creations manifest themselves physically . . . faster! Most of the time now, I can have my creations come alive physically within days, if not hours. But I digress, so back to the creation of my fences. At the time I didn't have the money to buy the fences and a tack house. I just had the creation of the fences planted firmly in my mind. I did however have a pop-up camping trailer for sale, which I had advertised in the newspaper. Within a week or so of creating my fences and continually holding the image of my creation in my mind, I got a call from a person wanting to buy my trailer. The man who called said he didn't have any money, but asked if I would be interested in trading my trailer for his services. I asked what he did and . . . yep, you guessed it . . . he made and welded four-bar horse fences. He had all the materials and the labourers to get the job done. **The window had opened**! I said I would love to trade my trailer for his four-bar horse fences, and the deal was done. And just a few weeks later a company called wanting to trade my advertising services for a tack shed. Call it coincidence if you want, but to me it was the physical manifestation of my mind's creation, and I have hundreds of create and wait stories just like these.

A Leap Of Faith

So, as with religion, I am asking you to take a leap of faith and **create and wait**. You can have anything in the world that you want. Anything! I don't mean you can raise the dead, but you can get a promotion at work or a 100-acre ranch . . . if you want. You decide. It's like the old saying, 'Be careful what you wish for, you just might get it.' I mention this also because, consciously or not, you can also create some really unhappy things. I knew a woman who walked around the high school track every day. While she walked she spoke of how miserable she was and how much she hated her husband. There were no options for this woman; after months of miserable thinking, she divorced her husband and has remained miserable. So, yes, be careful what you create for yourself. The more you create, believing that you will indeed possess your creation, the more often and the more quickly you will have the creation of your mind and thinking made manifest physically.

I can't believe I am asking you to try this. You know

how I feel about hocus-pocus! I feel the same way about medicine men, psychics, fortune-tellers, voodoo, healers, priests and seers. But that said, this principle of creation works with 100 per cent results. I don't have it happen 50, 60 or 70 per cent of the time, it works 100 per cent of the time with 100 per cent accuracy. Try it, and just wait for the window of opportunity to open, because it must open. The universe has no choice but to give it to you. The hardest part is seeing when the window opens and being willing to jump in immediately it does. Remember, you can't hesitate, or the window of opportunity will slam shut! If you allow the window to open too many times without jumping in, it will stop opening. People say, 'He who hesitates is lost.' I say, 'He who hesitates is not only lost . . . but so are his powers to create.' Use it or lose it!

Work While You Sleep!
One more thing, remember what I said about your mind never sleeping? Use that fact to not only create by thinking and focusing on your creation just before falling asleep, but also as a way to solve difficult problems. Just do this. When you have a dilemma that

you find hard to resolve, say to yourself, just as you are falling asleep at night, 'While I am sleeping I will have my mind work on this problem and when I awake I will have the answer!' It is kind of like having an operation. You go into the operating theatre, they put you to sleep, and when you wake up you have had major surgery - and all you did was sleep. Your mind has the equivalent of thousands of doctors working full-time to solve your problems while you are asleep. If you let your mind work on them, you will have the solution to your problems when you wake up. After all, eight hours is a long time to think about something without coming up with a solution. This works for creating, inventing, problem solving, business solutions, family problems, love problems, money problems, and all the normal concerns of everyday life. All you need do is 'sleep on it.'

Create and wait and sleep on it! That's it! This talent of using your mind is just like playing the piano. At first it is hard and seems impossible, but the longer and harder you practise, the easier and more fun it becomes. I am not asking you to believe me . . . just be a pragmatic thinking scientist and experiment with this principle, or law of the universe. What will it hurt?

I might just be right (and I assure you I am). If I am not right . . . you will have some imaginary fun and you will get lots of sleep. How bad can that be? Think about it.

8

Wishing vs. Doing

Now that we have talked a little about the hocus-pocus of business, which is anything but hocus-pocus, it's time to get real. This does not mean that you should stop using the create and wait principle: you must continue to do that. It is a principle used by all successful business people, whether they use it consciously or not. You never stop the process. When I say, 'Get real', I mean you need to understand the difference between 'wishers' and 'doers'. Creating is *not* wishing! But 'doing' does not always mean doing something physically. Thinking and creating are 'doing' too. Let's talk about a philosophy I call Fantasyland vs. Realityland.

The Sixth Requirement
Is it more fun to live in Fantasyland or Realityland? The Buddha said (and I paraphrase for my own selfish purposes), 'The problem with reality is that all life is

suffering.' The Laughing Buddha said that in order to have what he called a good life you must have self-mastery, a happy demeanour, purposeful endeavour, a deep commitment to the welfare of others, and enlightened awareness. How many out of those five do you have? Interesting . . . I think that in addition to the five items from the Laughing Buddha, there might be a sixth requirement. I think that you have got to have a fantasy or a dream – something you may never obtain, but which you would like to have and enjoy thinking about having.

To Fantasize . . .
Webster's Dictionary defines 'fantasy' as, 'the power or process of creating especially unrealistic or improbable mental images in response to psychological need.' I find that interesting. I have heard philosophers say that without a fantasy, man cannot be happy and is a miserable creature. In order to think about this fantasy question the way I am beginning to think about it, we have got to look at all the synonyms so we can understand the full scope of this idea, and don't get mixed up. A fantasy (at least for this discussion) is synonymous with a dream, an aspiration, a wish, a

longing, an ambition and a goal, just to name a few. They are all words representing what we want to happen (or think we want to happen) that hasn't happened yet. But fantasy, by any other name, is still a fantasy. It is something we want, or think we need, or have hope of happening, or strive to have, or wish to have happen, or lust for, or set goals to some day achieve.

. . . Or Not To Fantasize

However, unlike the philosophers who have said that in order for humans to be happy they must have a fantasy, I think that we are unhappy because of our fantasies. Having goals and ambitions and 'wishing and hoping and praying and dreaming' are the very causes of our unhappiness. All this longing and fantasizing and dreaming of having things we don't have, or of wanting certain things to happen which don't happen fast enough, is the very reason we can never be happy living in the present or in reality. Reality stinks compared with a life of dreams and fantasies. I contend that fantasy (and all the words we use to describe it) is the very thing that makes us unhappy with our lives, our jobs, our spouses, our friends, our kids, our homes . . . and all of our realities. We love being in the drunken state of Fantasyland. Fantasy is the drug of life. It is so addictive that it eventually rules our lives, creating a need for more and more fantasy to keep the buzz alive. We truly can't be happy without a new, and many times bigger, fantasy. Men want women they have never had and lust for, or fantasize about so much that they leave their wives to possess them, and when they do possess them, and the fantasy becomes reality, they start another fantasy all over again, because the reality is never quite as good as the fantasy. Women behave similarly.

However, it is not just in our love lives that the fantasy drug presents its addictive nature. We use fantasy every day to escape the realities of life. We rely on this drug every time we say, 'I will be happy when . . .'. We all do it. We start at a very early age and we never outgrow our need for the speed of fantasy. Whether it involves getting your first bike, going to college, graduating, getting a proper job, buying a house, buying the car you want, getting married, having children, getting divorced – it goes on and on. The funny thing is, just like taking cocaine, we really are happy for a while when our fantasy becomes reality, at least the mind thinks we are. The happiness lasts a few days or weeks, but after a while the drug slowly wears off. Eventually it stops working and we want more, and now we must have a new fantasy in order to be happy again.

Not The Past Or The Future . . .

I used to like to go to the shopping mall, to wish for things that someday I hoped to have. I have all those things now, and it's no longer fun to go to the mall. I have run out of fantasy stuff to possess. The reality is that I own all the things I used to think would make me happy. All of them gave me happiness for a while, but most of them are now in boxes in a storage unit to make room for more fantasy stuff to buy to make me happy. The drug of fantasy worship doesn't stop there. In order to escape the sorrows of reality, one must do one of two things, either create a fantasy for the future, or try to relive a fantasy of the past. As I observe people, as they grow older, they love to tell stories about the past. The past, you see, has long ago moved from the reality of present to the fantasy of past. We tell the stories of the past as if they were real, but they too are just a dream; a dream or fantasy being brought to life again to make the present more interesting. You know these people. They are still telling you stories about what they did in high school or college. These stories are no more real than the future fantasy stories that little kids tell you about becoming firemen or policemen when they grow up. It is no different from playing with an imaginary friend named Roger. A fantasy cannot be a fantasy in the here and now. Fantasies can't exist in the present, or they would be called reality. But they are fantasy . . . the drug of happiness. Yet the happiness created by fantasies is short lived, or worse, if they are never realized, they create sadness and discontent. Now, at least, I can see fantasy for what it really is, a despicable drug that I, and so many others, are addicted to. I have decided to quit fantasy and its let downs, and allow myself to love life in the present.

. . . Now!

So how does one live joyfully and happily in the present reality? Well, if fantasies eventually make you unhappy, wouldn't the lack of fantasies make you happy? Doesn't that make sense? What if you were just to live in the present with no expectations? What if you were just to get up in the morning and live? To do just what you needed to do, when you needed to do it, and do what you wanted to do, when you wanted to do it, and live in the reality of the moment, with no other expectation than just to live? Wouldn't that make you happy? What if you were to live life with no desire or attachment, with no fantasy of what might be, with no wish for something that may or may not happen, and with only one thing on your mind . . . live now? Wouldn't that make you happier? But maybe this is like telling a cocaine addict he would be much happier without cocaine. He would think you were crazy.

I've been trying this experiment for several years now, and I seem to be much happier. Sure bad things have happened, but bad things happen. A lot of good things have happened, but good things happen too. I have never been so productive. I am productive without even trying, because to try would require creating a fantasy, and living a productive life requires living now . . . and nothing more. The world is upside down, isn't it? We must allow life to do its own thing, and we must be like water on our downhill journey to the sea. Wouldn't it be silly for water to try and control its direction and flow uphill? But at least now, I can see fantasy for what it really is and remove it from my life.

I allow life to happen. Trying to control life is almost as silly as being an impatient farmer, who plants his field with corn and then goes out several times a day and yells at the ground, 'Grow, damn you, grow!' The corn will grow at its own speed. Sure you must water it and take care of it, but the corn knows how to grow. So it is with life. Allow life to grow at its own speed. It's a much more happy way to live. Now, I may be wrong, but what would it hurt to give my words a try? Hey, if it doesn't work for you, go back to living in Fantasyland. Realityland is not for those of weak character. Almost everyone wants the drug the dealers sell in Fantasyland, but if you can . . . just say no.

Wishing And Doing
There is a huge difference between the 'wishers' and the 'doers' of the world. Even though we allow life to happen, we never stop striving to make things happen. We are in control of our life not by wishing and saying, 'I will be happy when . . . ' We are in control of our life by creating and waiting, by doing the do, and allowing

the windows of opportunity to open for us and knowing that if we don't take action, nothing will happen. After all is said and done, the definition of being crazy is doing the same thing over and over again and expecting a different result each time. We have to change in order to be successful business people. We have to live with our feet firmly planted in Realityland.

We don't wish our way to success, we know the system, the principles, the way, the how to become rich, stay rich, and be happy in the process. It is only then that we will be full of joy and happiness as all of our most incredible dreams come true. Think about it.

Successful and Unsuccessful Applications of Pillar One

Enough of the technical nuts and bolts of how to get rich and stay rich. Let's take a look at some real-life applications of the four pillars, beginning with the successful and unsuccessful applications of Pillar One. In all cases, I am using real-life businesses and business people, whom I know and have worked with, to illustrate the differences. Only the names have been changed to protect the not-so-innocent.

Turn Business Away?!
When I first started my advertising agency in Mesa, Arizona, I was approached by a young, aggressive chiropractor who wanted to increase his business through advertising, so we started working together. After a short period, his business started to boom. He had more work than he knew what to do with. So what did he do? Rather than hiring more people when he was 60 to 70 per cent busy, he got to where he was

110 per cent busy and so he did the only logical thing. He stopped advertising. He had so much business that in order to keep up, he needed less business. You see, if he had less business he could keep up with all his appointments and still have time to play golf on Thursday mornings.

It is a fact that businesses can't stay the same. Your business is either going to increase or decrease. More firms go out of business with too much work than with too little. The reason for this is that too much business, if not handled correctly, actually turns customers and clients away. For example, I went into an electronics store the other day and they had so many customers and so few checkout aisles and employees that even though I wanted and needed to buy something there, I put my item back on the shelf and walked out. They had too much business to handle. In time, too much business will lead to fewer and fewer customers and clients who will put up with the inconvenience. Our generation expects everything *now* . . . so time is of the essence.

Time To Share

I went to a restaurant about two years ago where the

food was the best I have ever eaten. The friends I was with raved about the taste and presentation, but none of us would ever go back. Because even though we had reservations for 7:30 pm it was 8:30 pm before we got in and then it took 50 minutes to serve us. By then we were so mad that even the quality of the food didn't make up for the delays. Too much business can actually produce much less if you don't handle the increase effectively. This particular restaurant was a ticking time bomb. During the two years they were open, despite the quality of the food, they gradually had fewer and fewer people willing to put up with the long waits, resulting in a decrease in clientele. They are no longer serving 100 people a night, they aren't serving anyone any more. They are out of business because they had too much business and refused to figure out how to handle it. That's why I tell you; when you are 60 to 70 per cent busy, it is time to share the knowledge.

When To Hire?
Here's one more piece of advice. It is easy to be in business for one or two years. But it's hard to be in business for five years and more. There is a cycle that

all businesses go through. You start with a new business, then you become established, and you end up with an old business. It is then time to recreate your business. Make it new again, or you will be out of business. Having a new business is the easiest part of the cycle. When you become established, life becomes confusing. You are making enough money to get by, but not enough money to be rich. You are working hard, but you have reached a financial plateau. It is at this point that you have to decide whether to go for it and expand your business by hiring new people and buying new equipment, or to try to hold on to what you've got and hope the business doesn't slow down. Remember, it can't stay the same. It is either going to grow or start to die. It is at this go-for-it point with an established business that you could also lose your shirt. If you increase your overhead by hiring more people with the expectation of more business you could start to lose money fast! This is like walking on a razor's edge. You cannot grow your business if you don't hire new people and share the knowledge. Many times, you cannot grow your business if you don't buy new equipment, get a bigger office, buy more inventories, borrow more money, decrease your profit margin for a while, and risk killing the goose that lays the golden eggs. However, if business does not increase and billings go up while net profits go down, you may be out of business fast.

Not 'Great For The Price' – Just 'Great'!

In Pillar One, if you are as good as the competition at the same price as the competition, you have cause to worry. But when your business is twice as good at half the price, and you have figured out how to make money with this business model, your risk is not as great. Expanding your business is made simpler when the question 'if not you, who?' has no other 'who'. Removing the other 'who' isolates you from bad times or even stupid mistakes you may make in your expansion. Keep working hard to be twice as good at half the price. A good example of this came from one of my business mentors who owned a pizza franchise. We will call him Tom. He owned 33 large pizza stores in the south-west USA. I was in a benchmark meeting with him when one of his managers said, 'We make a great pizza for the price.' 'What did you say?' Tom yelled. The manager repeated his statement. Tom looked him right in the eye and said, 'Listen, I never want to hear you say that again. That is a sure way for us to go out of business. We don't make a great pizza for the price . . . We make a great pizza no matter what the price!' and they did! Even though the business positioning of the pizza business was to sell large pizzas for only $3.95 while others were selling the same pizza for $12.95 and more, Tom wanted to make sure that the quality of the pizza was not less just because they charged less. He knew that in order to have a great business he wanted his customers to want his pizza more than those of their competitors. He was not content to make a pizza that was 'great for the price,' he wanted to sell his customers a great pizza. Charging $3.95 had nothing to do with the quality of the pizza. I learned a real business lesson at that meeting. Regardless of what you charge for your product or services you must never sacrifice quality because you charge less. If you do, it is harder to get and keep clients and customers.

Sales, Sales, Sales . . .
Now, many don't have the courage or stupidity, whichever it may be, to be entrepreneurs and start

their own business, and it is hard to be twice as good at half the price if you are working for someone. This doesn't mean that you can't get rich, but you have to go about it in a different way. The easiest way is to start your own business because then you have 100 per cent control over your own destiny. I have always found this to be the best way for me. But if you like what you do and enjoy the job you have, and are lucky enough to be working for an entrepreneur, then you too have a great opportunity to get rich. Entrepreneurs love money. They love it when their employees want to make them more money. They are always excited when an employee comes to their office and says, 'I have a new idea about how we might be able to make even more money here.' There is no faster way to get their attention. So, look at the business where you are now employed and look at how the money is made. It will boil down to two areas; sales and service. New business must be sold, and existing accounts, clients and customers must be serviced well to keep them. That boils down to sales, too. You are continually selling to your existing accounts to keep them as existing accounts, clients and customers.

. . . And More Sales!

So it really boils down to only one thing you can offer
. . . more sales. Sales are the life-blood of all
companies. If you can show your boss how he or she
can make more sales, they will drop everything they
are doing and give you their time. New ideas for
increased sales are what make the entrepreneurial
world go round. The problem is that when it comes to
ideas, it is like the avocado. I love the taste of
avocados, but a lot of people don't. It is not the
avocado that tastes good or bad, an avocado just is!
But liking it is a matter of personal taste – you either
like it or you don't, and so it is with ideas. Many of the
ideas you come up with to increase sales may be good
ideas, but when presented to your boss, they may not
like the 'taste' of the idea. So don't take it personally if
the boss doesn't think it will make money. All you need
to do, at first, is think. Constantly be thinking of new
ideas, new systems, new products, new concentrations,
new markets, new services, and so on, that will make
more money for your company, and consistently talk
with your boss about these ideas. I want to tell you
that in my life of ideas, it is the old 80/20 rule – that
is, that only 20 per cent of ideas are any good. A full

80 per cent will be left on the cutting-room floor. So again, don't think you are stupid when you come up with an idea that your boss doesn't think will work. Just keep on thinking and soon you will be the 'listening ear' for your boss. Keep the conversation open in a friendly, 'I'm a part of your team' way and you will be surprised what will happen. Pretty soon you will walk into your boss's office with one of your money-making ideas and they will say, 'I like it' and look out . . . here comes rich! Remember, your ideas must centre around how your boss can make more money! Tell him or her that you want to be the one to make it happen and show them your plan to make both of you more money. You have to be in control of the sale of your new idea. Sales people always make three to five times more money than service people. Blood (sales) is more important than fat (service) at most companies. The fat is the first to go when times get hard and the company must be skinny. Sales people are the last to go. The boss has to decide that he or she will start doing the selling again on their own, which most bosses don't have time to do, for the sales people to be let go. So you must move into a sales position of some kind, as quickly as you can, hopefully

selling your new idea and making money for the company. Just because you don't want to start your own company, doesn't mean you can't get rich and follow the same four pillars of wealth. Your idea for making the boss and the company more money will still have to be twice as good at half the price if you want to sell your product or service more quickly and easily, and keep your clients longer and more profitably. Your sales ideas must always centre on the first pillar, twice as good at half the price.

Get Your Part Of The Action

I know a man who is a production director at an advertising agency. It is his job to make sure that all the TV spots, radio spots, long-form videos, dubs, shoots and so on get done on time with quality production. He manages a team of about 15 producers, editors and production personnel. He is also in charge of editing all the radio spots, and is one of the best editors of radio spots and audio I have ever seen. The problem is that he is too good. The agency directors don't want him to do anything except edit radio spots and run the production department. The trouble with this is that the production director's job, along with the radio editor's job, was a financial dead end. Even though he is paid well, there is only so much the directors of an agency can pay for a production director and a radio editor. Many of the video editors are getting paid much more than he is, which is the case in many companies. Similarly, the sales managers at most companies make less than most of the sales people. If you are not bringing money in to the company and are just managing the real producers of revenue, then you get paid well, but not as much as the sales leaders. So, for this production director to find himself in the same predicament as many sales managers was not atypical. If you want to get rich you must find a way to get part of the action. You must come up with an idea to get a percentage of the net profit or you will eventually reach a point in your career at which you have 'topped out.' You will make good money, but you can't get rich because there is only so much companies can pay for non-revenue producing jobs. Remember the rule: twice as good at half the price. The same rule holds true for 'as good at the same price.' If you are as good at the same price there comes a point when you ask for money and your boss will have a choice. He or she can give you the money you ask for, or hire someone as good as you at less than you are asking. The choice will be very clear to the boss. Hire a new you! So if you want to make more money for you, make more money for the company and get a piece of the action!

Sell The Idea

So, back to the production director. He went to the boss and said, 'I need to make more money and here is what I think we can do to make you (the boss) more money and allow me to make more money at the same time.' At this point he had the boss's attention. So he continued, 'I want to sell more business for our production department over and above the business we currently have. I have a plan to sell this increased business by doing TV spots for the local cable system. They are always saying that they could sell more if their production department could keep up with sales. I have talked to them and they want us to do their spots for them and will pay us $1500 per commercial. I can do this with the staff I currently have. We are only about 60 per cent busy, which means that without increasing overhead I can increase studio profit to the company. I will service the new business so we don't have to tie up our account servicing department with production-only business. This is pure profit for the company, and all I want is 10 per cent of it. What do you think?' Well, needless to say, there is a new business in town under the umbrella of the parent company called The Studios. In addition to the cable company business, the production director has also brought in work from other advertising agencies, in-house agencies, marketing directors and direct clients. Best of all, he now has permission from his directors to 'replace himself' while continuing to receive his salary as production director and radio editor. The directors now plan to increase the production department as a profit centre and expect the time to come when he will need to choose between doing the editing, or radio commercials and selling new production accounts. At this point, they expect him to hire someone to be the radio editor and oversee their production. Do you see what he will be ready to do in a short period of time? Yep, share the knowledge. He is well on his way to being rich. 'Sell the sale' to your boss and you are on your way to becoming rich. Think about it.

Successful and Unsuccessful Applications of Pillar Two

Pillar Two explains your need to **share the knowledge** if you want to get rich. This means you must become responsive, but not responsible, which I will explain at the end of this chapter. You would think that showing people what, how, when, and where you 'do your do' would be simple. Why wouldn't you be excited to show people how to do what you do so they can start doing it and allow you to do other things? But you would be surprised how many people can't slow down enough to share the knowledge. They allow their people to follow them around and observe what they do and hope they will learn. But that is like asking someone to sit in the cockpit with you and hope that one day they will know how to fly a 747. That would be stupid. When I say share the knowledge, I mean teach, and expect hands-on learning to occur. That means you have to slow down, be patient, bite your tongue a little and allow someone to make mistakes so they can become better than you at what you do. Most mentors, for some reason, feel they always need to be top dog, and be smarter and better than the people they are teaching. This is wrong! When I say share the knowledge, I'm saying it with the expectation that the people you are training to do what you do, will eventually be better than you.

Can't Teach, Won't Teach

At my advertising agency we have one of the fastest TV editors in the world. Without a doubt I have never seen an editor who could even come close to his speed and quality. He is easily twice as fast as any other editor, and the quality of his work has never suffered because of his speed. The problem is, he can't teach anyone how to be as good as he is. He can't be bothered with people who are slower or not as good as him. He can't sit back and let his students edit and push the buttons. Nope! It kills him to have that much patience. He says watch me and then ask me questions if you have any. But when someone asks a question he says, 'I really don't have time to explain that right now.' So when we want a new editor to be trained, we have to have a slower, more patient, less good editor do the training. That's just the way it is, and that is just the way it is with many entrepreneurs. They can't slow down enough to do the most important thing they must do if they want to get rich, which is to share the knowledge. Sad, but true. So these entrepreneurs will continue to do the do for the rest of their lives and make good money, but they will never get rich.

You have to be willing to slow down and share your knowledge until the person who is taking your place is better than you are, or you can't move on to the next pillar. If you try to move on to Pillar Three without completing Pillar Two, you are dead in the water. Sharing the wealth with others before they are better than you at what you do only means you will make less money. The people you teach and train have got to *earn* the right to receive the riches you want to share with them. You will know that it's time to share the wealth when, and only when, they are better than you at what you do. But be careful, you can take too long in sharing the knowledge and expecting your protégés to make the grade. If you are teaching a person who seems to be taking a long time to 'get it,' you may have the wrong person. You need to be wise enough to realize that that person will never measure up to the standard your clients and customers expect, and cut loose. The people you hire to make your company better need to be fast learners and hard workers. There are plenty of them out there, but you may have to look hard and expect much.

Know What You Are Good At

At our advertising agency we went through 10 to 15 people to head our new account development sales programme until we found the perfect person. She is one of our directors at the agency. If you are trying to put a square person in a round job, realize it early in the process. Don't keep trying to change the person or change the job. You will never be able to stop doing the do until you find the right person. I once asked an artist at the agency to head our public relations and corporate communications company. In my mind she was perfect for the job. She could have earned much more money in this position. Yet after a very short period of time, she was wise enough to say, 'I am an artist. I love being an artist. I don't want to be in public relations. I love to create and design great print ads. That's what I am all about. Thanks for the offer, but I am happy as a graphic artist and that's what I want to continue to be.' I really appreciated her honesty. She saved herself, the company, and me many months of frustration. Not all of us can be artists.

Not all of us are cut out to be managers. Not all of us can be happy doing any job. Most of us finally follow our hearts and choose what we want. Those are the wise and profitable people we want working for us. I could be a manager of a radio station. I have the knowledge and the drive, but every day of my life I would hate it. I am an entrepreneur and I know it. So it is with the people you hire to take your place and make you more money. They have got to want to be you. They have got to want to be better than you. They have got to get out of bed every morning and say, 'I love what I am doing. This is fun. I am the luckiest person in the world.' OK, that may be an exaggeration, but you get my point.

Money Or Fun?

We once hired a real estate agent to work for our real estate company. He made a great living, but that was not what he wanted to be. He told me that he wanted to be an artist and painter and that he was selling real estate to earn enough money to allow him to paint. Now, at first glance, this guy doesn't sound like someone with whom you would want to share the knowledge. Let's be logical here, many times we really don't know what we want to be in life. I was on the radio as a broadcaster and disc jockey for nearly 15 years. I loved it. I did it while I had other businesses. I would do my show from 6 am to 9:00 am and then go to work. I would still be on the radio if I could afford to be on the radio. But the time, energy and resources needed for me to stay on the radio were not worth the income. In order to make the kind of money I wanted I would have to move from market to market and I was not willing to do that. But to this day, when I listen to the radio I say, 'I could do that so much better.' Now the same thing holds true for many people just as it does for my real estate agent and me. What we *love* to do can never make enough money to afford the lifestyle we also want. Now I don't want to discourage all the painters and radio personalities, but sometimes you have to choose between money and fame. Sometimes you have to choose between money and fun. I chose money and to run businesses that are fun. So it was with my real estate agent friend. He came to me one day and said, 'I only want to paint for fun. I am having too much fun and making so much money in real estate that I want to be great in real estate and leave the painting for my free time. Will you take me under your wing and teach me?' Well, the rest is history. He now makes a great living in real estate. He loves what he is doing, but he no longer has time to sell and list. He now manages our real estate company and helps more than 100 other agents reach their goals. We shared the knowledge and he took that knowledge to build the company much bigger and more profitably than we could have done on our own.

Now, you need to be responsive but not responsible. This means you need to be **responsive** to the needs, questions, and concerns of your staff, but **not responsible for doing the do**. Once you have trained staff and shared your knowledge with them you must let them do the do or they will never really learn. Applied knowledge is real knowledge. Knowledge that is not applied is worthless. Knowing everything about swimming is no good unless you get in the water and swim.

Share your knowledge with your people and let them share this knowledge with others. Then you can make them rich and you will become even richer in the process. I mentioned before the saying, 'When the student is ready, the teacher will appear.' Well, I have a twist on that saying. I say, 'When the teacher is ready, the student will appear.' Not only do we need the right student to make Pillar Two work, we need the right teacher. You! Think about it.

Successful and Unsuccessful Applications of Pillar Three

Pillar Three, as you know, is the pillar where you **share the wealth**. At first you may think that sharing the wealth is for your student's or protégé's benefit. Although that may be a reason, it is not the **rich** reason. You are sharing the wealth so you can have more wealth. If you are not willing to share the wealth, you cannot get rich. It may seem a little paradoxical, but it is true. Sharing the wealth allows you to become richer, and the more you share the more rich you will become. Let me explain again. When you pay someone more than they would get paid doing the same job somewhere else, you assure that your managers and the leaders of your company won't leave you. These people that you have trained, taught, shared knowledge with, encouraged, and now trust, have got to know that they have a piece of the action. In addition to making a good income, they also participate in the net profits. The better they do, the more they make. Sure, they have got to love (or at least like) what they are doing, but most of the drop outs left you a long time ago. These people you have *want* to be working with and for you, and love what they are doing. So pay them well and they won't ever leave you. Remember, if your people leave you, you lose money. It would cost a fortune to start the process over again.

Keep Your Staff

I was doing some life coaching with a friend of mine who was complaining that he couldn't keep good people. He runs a landscaping company and was being hurt by companies who hired illegal immigrants and paid them next to nothing for their work. He said that landscaping was hard work and that finding people to do the job and manage manual labour was next to impossible. He wanted to know what I would do. I asked him how long it took him to train someone to do the landscaping jobs he did. He replied four to six weeks. So I said that if I understood correctly, this means it takes a new person four to six weeks to be up to maximum performance. He agreed. So I told him he was losing productivity every time he lost one of his workers, because of the time needed to train new people and get them up to speed. He told me that in the training period the workers worked more slowly, and time was money to him. He charged his clients a fixed fee and yet paid his workers by the hour. The slower they worked the more it cost him and the less he made. Time and performance were the keys to his income. So I told him that this was a 'no-brainer'. All he had to do was keep his people longer and he would make more money. Pretty simple. Of course he wanted to know how to do that so I said, pay them more. To which he replied he was already paying the going rate. To which I responded, **pay them more**. Pay them double what they can make anywhere else and they will never leave you. They will even recruit for you. They will tell all their friends about you and your company and you will never lack workers. So we did the sums, and much to my friend's dismay, the numbers didn't lie. Hiring and rehiring, loss of production, loss of business due to shabby work, always starting anew, never knowing from day to day if he was going to have to do the work himself to get the job done, not being able to expand and grow his business, cost my friend much more money than just paying his people more (and hopefully a lot more) than they could make anywhere else doing the same thing. The by-product is that when workers stay longer, the leaders and managers rise up to take your place, so you can stop sharing the knowledge and start enjoying sharing the wealth – so you can become richer.

Make Them Happy Before They Ask

When people leave you, it costs you much more than just paying more for them to stay. When you give the managers and leaders of your company the ability to make even more by having a share of the profits they will think twice about leaving you even on the bad days, and will enjoy their jobs even more. Here is a secret of success: **give them more before**! One of the rules of sharing the wealth is to give it freely *before* they ask for it. I consulted just recently with a company whose policy was to not pay their people more unless they asked for it. Then they would only pay them half as much as they asked for. The logic was that they had hired them for a certain amount and why should they pay more than that? After all, the person had agreed to work for that amount. **But just like so many companies, they were constantly**

complaining about the high turnover of their employees. They had a 143 per cent employee turnover. I know that sounds unbelievable, but it is a fact. I am here to tell you that you can't have a 143 per cent employee turnover and expect to make money. You will spend all your time hiring and training. And even more of a problem was that the people who did stay were the C and D level workers. They couldn't keep the A and B level workers. They fired the F level workers – those who didn't and wouldn't work. They are easy to fire. So what this C and D employee retention meant was that the work was getting done poorly, slowly, sloppily and inefficiently, turning off more customers and clients than they were turning on. Their customer satisfaction index was below 40 per cent. Is it any wonder? All the good employees, managers and leaders left. They wanted more money and other companies were willing to pay more. So, give them more before! When an employee decides to leave it is too late to pay them more. They are out of the door! They have moved on. Don't make your people spend their lunch hours looking for a new job. Pay them more and they will give you more.

I am now consulting with a company which has the

policy, 'there are more where they came from.' What they mean is that a monkey could do their jobs. If one monkey doesn't want to work there, there are lots more monkeys in the jungle. They are partially right. For the kind of low-skill, low-expectation, manual labour jobs they offer, you don't need to be able to think your way out of a paper bag. But even in these kinds of jobs, if you pay your staff more, you will eventually find people that have the 'fire in their belly.' They will become some of your most loyal employees and sometimes, even your good friends. There is nothing more gratifying to me than to give people a leg up and see them excel and become great. It doesn't happen every time, but it happens more than you would think. So the bottom line is, if you want to increase your bottom-line profits, pay your people more. Try to pay them twice as much as they could make doing the same job somewhere else and they will make you rich. Think about it.

12

Successful and Unsuccessful Applications of Pillar Four

As I have told you before, this is the hardest pillar to do correctly; but you can never be rich until you understand the principles of the fourth pillar. The reason this pillar is so difficult to understand, master and apply, is that people try to get there too fast or never quite get there at all. Either way, you cannot get rich. Let me explain.

One Step At A Time
I consult with a company that attempted to bypass Pillar One and move as fast as possible to Pillar Four. These businessmen forgot about the rule Pillar One explains: you can't share the knowledge or share the wealth until *you*, mainly through your own efforts, are 70 per cent busy and realize that if you don't get some help soon you will be 100 per cent busy and unable to grow. They developed a good idea and immediately hired people to sell it. They hired people to service the

clients before they had really ironed out all the problems. They hadn't developed systems to avoid human error, and they hadn't made enough mistakes to be able to tell others what *not* to do. You can't jump from Pillar One to Pillar Four before you are ready. You will get stuck in the cement of business and won't be able to claw your way out. You are setting yourself up for failure in a short period of time.

If you are just 10 per cent busy and then try to stop doing the do (Pillar Four), hoping someone you hire will do it instead, you are kidding yourself. You don't have a real company. You have to *prove* that you have a real company *before* you go hiring someone to share your knowledge and share your wealth. *You* have to do the do long enough to enable you to share your knowledge with your people, in addition to sharing some of the work and responsibility with them so you can grow. If all you want is to hire an assistant who does all your work so you can play golf every day, you have not listened to what I am telling you. You have to do the do until you have to share the work, responsibility, accountability and knowledge with someone else to prevent you from working 18-hour days and dying of a heart attack at 45. Believe me, when that time comes, you will know. You won't have to ask anyone.

Sell The Sale
Here at Pillar Four, it is time for you to do only one thing. Sell the sale! That's right; all you will do is get more business for your company. You are the salesperson who gets the business so that others can do the do and you can get rich. I think it is important that you don't forget to sell the sale and try to turn this responsibility over to an employee. You need to hear what people are saying, answer objections, negotiate contracts, set appointments, develop marketing tools and collateral materials, and so on. You need to be the best sales person for your service or product. However, remember that sales is all you really do. You will have others who run the business for you and service your clients. After a while, when you are too busy selling the sale, you will need to hire a salesperson with whom you will share the knowledge and share the wealth. You will know when it is time to hire this person when you know that you are 'leaving money on the table.' When you know that a professionally trained salesperson like yourself could

help you double or triple your sales, it is time to hire. It won't cost you money, because you are losing money if you don't hire someone. When you are 70 to 80 per cent busy and know there is much more business potential out there, hire someone.

Time To Stop Doing The Do

At some point, when sales are great and the person, or persons, you have hired are selling plenty without you, you can stop selling and **stop doing the do** altogether. You can then become chairman of the board and have your leaders, directors and managers report to you so you can give them guidance and counsel on how to run the company. You will set benchmarks for them to achieve and will work hard with them to help them accomplish the goals of the company. But remember, you do nothing. As I mentioned earlier, I have a sign on my desk that says, 'I want my companies and the people who work for my companies to get as much done today as can possibly be done *without me doing anything*!' and that is not easy. You will want to step in and tell your leaders and directors how to do their jobs, or worse, you will step in and start doing the do. Remember, if you have done your job right, you are worse at doing the do than your people. Remember you trained them and shared the knowledge so that they would be better than you. Don't rehire yourself; you're not as good as they are. You need to be a great chairman because you are a lousy doer. If you are tempted to rehire yourself because your people are not doing a good enough job, that means that you didn't do a good enough job of sharing the knowledge with your people. Think about it.

13

Take the Ball and Run With It

There you have it: a lot of hard work, a little hocus pocus, and Four Pillars of Wealth that cannot fail. This formula and system will work for any business no matter how big or small, no matter if the business has been in existence for years or months. No matter what, this system works 100 per cent of the time. It has been proven by tens of thousands of businesses and has never failed.

Whatever Your Lifestyle – Be Rich
I wrote this book to help people get rich, if they want to. How rich you want to be is up to you. I have never thought that money solved that many problems. Many times it creates more problems than solutions. The only thing that having money does is allow a person to stop worrying about money. Remember, rich is not a figure, it's a lifestyle. Being rich means a different figure and a different lifestyle for each and every one of us. You

decide the figure and you decide the lifestyle. But be rich. Being a successful entrepreneur requires a lot of hard work . . . but it is worth it. Owning, leading, and managing your own business or the business of others is hard work . . . but it is worth it. Having enough patience to share the knowledge is hard work . . . but it is worth it. Having enough faith to share the wealth, making you rich, is hard to do . . . but it is worth it. Working hard every day to get as much done as possible without your doing anything is hard to do . . . but it is worth it. You can do this. Don't let fear keep you from becoming rich. Don't let impatience keep you from becoming rich. Don't let greed keep you from becoming rich. Don't let pride keep you from becoming rich.

You can have whatever you want. You cannot fail! This is *your* new beginning! **Take the ball and run with it**! Being rich is a good thing! Think about it.

The Author

Larry John is a businessman, author, life coach, thinker, and founder of the website 'The Pragmatic Thinker' (www.thepragmaticthinker.com). Larry was born in Mesa, Arizona, in 1948. He is the son of Charles Floyd John and Opal John. He was almost literally born into the advertising and broadcast business. From the age of three he was singing and performing for family and friends. At the age of five, he became a weekly regular on a local Phoenix TV and radio show, *The Lew King Ranger Show*. Larry sang, tap-danced, acted, announced, and did live commercials until the age of 16, when he fell in love with rock 'n' roll. He loved music and played drums, guitar, piano, bass, and sang in local bands in the Phoenix area during his teenage years. Larry started playing drums at age 10 in a Dixieland band, The Mesa Imps, and continued to play in bands for over 30 years. He still plays from time to time.

Larry received a music-drama scholarship to Arizona

State University, which he attended for two years. His last two years of college were spent at Brigham Young University in Utah, where he received his B.A. degree in broadcasting. During his college years in Utah, Larry played in rock and country bands and performed for 10 years on his own TV show, *Hotel Balderdash*, in Salt Lake City. During that time he was also a local morning radio personality on various radio stations and owned his own newspaper, *The Desert Gazette*. It was also during this time in Utah that Larry started his own advertising agency.

Larry also has a great interest in real estate. He became a real estate broker and started his own real estate company. In 1982 Larry and his family returned to Arizona where he created Larry John Advertising and Public Relations. In 1984, he joined forces with his lifetime friend and attorney, John Wright, to form Larry John Wright Advertising, Inc., Larry John Wright Real Estate, Inc., John Wright Sales and Marketing, Larry John Wright Morales Hispanic Advertising, Inc., and the L-K Livestock Company. In 1998, Larry started his daily syndicated radio show, *Larry John and the Hot Tub Radio Party*, which played on as many as 25 radio stations for three years.

Larry John Wright has a staff of nearly 50 professionals and has advertising and marketing clients in over 200 markets nationwide. LJW has offices and broadcast and graphic arts studios in Phoenix, with branch offices in Salt Lake City, San Diego and Philadelphia.

In addition to being a businessman, in 2001 Larry became a professional life coach. As a life coach he advises and consults with individuals and businesses to help them clearly define and achieve their goals.

In 2003, Larry was inducted into the Arizona Broadcasters' Association Hall of Fame, honouring him for his contributions for over 50 years in broadcasting and advertising.

Larry has enjoyed writing for many years, and in addition to his Pragmatic Thinking commentaries, writes a weekly newspaper column on real estate for the *Arizona Tribune*, and five weekly radio and television shows called *Take a Minute to Think About It*, which are syndicated to various markets throughout the nation.

Larry and his wife Michal have been married over 30 years and have seven children: Jessica, Sam, Joe, Preston, David, Kim and Jackie. They also have ten grandchildren. Larry and Michal each have their own personal Harley-Davidson motorbike, and enjoy riding as much as possible. Larry has been known to say, 'If I die on my Harley, it's a great way to go!'

Larry and Michal love their home in Lehi, Arizona, a 'cowboy' community just north of Mesa. They also spend as much time as they can at their home in Maui and at their Rendezvous Ranch in Northern Arizona, where they breed Rocky Mountain horses and enjoy the Arizona skies.

Acknowledgements

Let me start by expressing my heartfelt gratitude to my wife and partner of 31 years, Michal, for her constant support and dedication towards helping me write this book. Without her help and guidance, the book would not have been possible. She spent hour upon hour of her time checking the contents to make sure that each detail I wished to explain was understandable. She is a great partner. I also want to thank my children: Jessica, Sam, Joe, Preston, David, Kim and Jackie for their encouragement to write this book. They reminded me often that it needed to be written. They reminded me of the fact that in most cases, 'the cobblers' children have no shoes.' They wanted to make sure that they and their children had my thoughts about the wonderful world of entrepreneurship and business in writing.

I also want to give my appreciation to my business partner of over 20 years, John Wright, for his support.

He allowed me the time it takes to write a book and the resources of our company to get the project done. I would also like to thank Scott Anderson, my long-time friend and associate, for his support and guidance. Scott not only helped encourage me to get this book published, but he is also the voice and on-screen talent for my radio and TV show, *Take a Minute to Think About It*. Of course I want to acknowledge the proof-reading talent of Mary Anderson, who gave countless hours of her time proof-reading and offering technical suggestions. I also acknowledge the talent of Sarah Carter, who served as my chief editor. She tried to make sure that the content and information in this book was well written while still keeping the flavour of the information. I'd also like to thank Katie John for all of her input. When it came to business and money I owe so much to my uncle, Arthur Reeve Beals. Reeve knew more about money than anyone I have ever met and he passed on a little of that knowledge to me. I thank him for that.

Last, but certainly not least, I want to express my appreciation and love to my Mom and Dad, Opal and Floyd John. Mom raised me to question everything. She loved to read and enjoyed 'thinking outside the box.'

She loved life and all people. She was truly one of the wisest people I have ever met. She had a heart as big as the world and a brain to match. Dad taught me the importance of working hard. He taught me this as we were digging ditches every night after dinner. Chopping the weeds in the ditch and talking about life, he taught me many lessons that I still hold dear to this day. Dad loved and respected hard-working businessmen and entrepreneurs and admired their accomplishments. No greater parents ever lived.

Index